THINK AND BECOME WEALTHY FOR MEN AT 30

Mastering Financial And Personal Growth In Your Thirties

Spencer Ryan Maxwell

Table of Contents

CHAPTER ONE 4
   DEFINING SUCCESS AT 30 4
   UNDERSTANDING THE IMPORTANCE OF SETTING GOALS AND ASPIRATIONS IN YOUR 30S 7

CHAPTER TWO 11
   EXPLORING THE POWER OF POSITIVE THINKING AND MINDSET MASTERY FOR SUCCESS 14

CHAPTER THREE 18
   THE ART OF PERSISTENCE 18
   LEARNING TO PERSEVERE THROUGH CHALLENGES AND SETBACKS ON THE PATH TO SUCCESS 21

CHAPTER FOUR 25
   BUILDING STRONG RELATIONSHIPS 25
   NURTURING PERSONAL AND PROFESSIONAL RELATIONSHIPS TO SUPPORT YOUR JOURNEY 28
   FINANCIAL INTELLIGENCE 31

CHAPTER FIVE 35
   HEALTH IS WEALTH 35
   PRIORITIZING PHYSICAL AND MENTAL WELL-BEING FOR SUSTAINED SUCCESS 37
   LEADERSHIP AND INFLUENCE 40

CHAPTER SIX 44
   TURNING ADVERSITY INTO ADVANTAGE 44
   GOAL SETTING AND ACTION PLANNING 47

CRAFTING A MEANINGFUL LEGACY THAT TRANSCENDS
FINANCIAL SUCCESS..51

THE END 55

CHAPTER ONE
DEFINING SUCCESS AT 30

Success at 30 is about setting personal goals and achieving them by this age. It means being happy with what you've accomplished, but still wanting more. Success isn't just about money or status; it's about feeling fulfilled and happy in different areas of life.

First, success at 30 involves doing well in your career. By this age, many people want to be established in their job, whether that means moving up in a company, starting their own business, or following a passion. It's about feeling good at what you do and enjoying your work.

Financial stability is also important. By 30, many aim to be financially independent, able to support themselves comfortably, and plan for the future. This could mean paying off debts, saving for big goals like buying a house or starting a family, and investing for long-term security.

Success at 30 also includes personal growth and relationships. It's about understanding yourself better, knowing your strengths and weaknesses, and always trying to improve. Building strong relationships with friends, family, and romantic partners is crucial, as these connections bring joy and support.

Health and well-being are key parts of success. By 30, taking care of your physical and mental health becomes more important. This means regular exercise, eating well, getting enough sleep, and managing stress. Having a positive mindset and being able to handle life's challenges is also essential.

Additionally, success at 30 involves having a sense of purpose and giving back to society. This could be through volunteer work, charity, or simply being a good person and helping your community. Making a positive impact adds meaning to your life.

In the end, success at 30 is different for everyone. It's about aligning your actions with your values and feeling content with where you are in life. It's recognizing that success is a journey, not a destination, and always striving for growth, happiness, and fulfillment in all areas of life.

UNDERSTANDING THE IMPORTANCE OF SETTING GOALS AND ASPIRATIONS IN YOUR 30S

In your 30s, setting goals is really important. This is a time when many people have settled into their jobs, relationships, and personal lives. The choices you make now can greatly affect your future. Here's why having goals matters:

1. Direction and Focus: Goals give you a clear path to follow, like a map for your life. Without goals, you might feel lost or unsure about where you're going.

Goals help you stay focused on what's important to you.

2. Personal Growth: Your 30s are a great time for growing and learning. Setting goals pushes you to learn new things and try new experiences. Whether it's getting better at your job, improving your health, or following a passion, goals help you become the best you can be.

3. Motivation and Accountability: Goals keep you motivated, especially when things get tough. When you know what you want to achieve, it's easier to stay driven and overcome challenges. Also, sharing your goals with others can help keep you accountable and provide support.

4. Financial Security: Financial stability becomes more important in your 30s. Setting financial goals, like saving for a house, paying off debt, or investing for retirement, helps you secure your future. Without clear financial goals, managing money can be harder and you might miss out on important opportunities.

5. Work-Life Balance: Balancing work and personal life can be tricky as your responsibilities grow. Setting goals for work-life balance helps you focus on what matters most. Whether it's spending time with family, enjoying hobbies, or taking care of your health, setting boundaries and goals can lead to a more balanced life.

6. Legacy and Impact: Your 30s are a good time to think about the mark you want to leave and the difference you want to make. Setting goals that match your values helps you create a meaningful life that positively affects others. Whether through your job, community, or relationships, having goals that reflect your values can make your life more fulfilling.

CHAPTER TWO
MASTERING YOUR MINDSET

1. Clear Goals: Know exactly what you want. Define your goals clearly. Whether it's building a big business, earning a certain amount of money, or gaining assets, being clear about your goals is essential.

2. Strong Desire: Have a strong desire for your goals. It's more than just wanting success; you need to be passionate about it. This desire helps you stay determined and keep taking action.

3. Believe in Yourself: Trust yourself and believe you can achieve your goals. Have faith in your vision, even when

things get tough. Keep believing that you will succeed in the end.

4. Positive Self-Talk: Use positive affirmations and self-talk to program your mind for success. Replace negative thoughts with positive ones like "I am capable," "I deserve success," and "I attract good things easily."

5. Learn and Grow: Always learn more about your field. Become an expert in your area. Find mentors, take courses, and use resources to expand your knowledge and skills. Knowledge is powerful, especially when used well.

6. Use Your Imagination: Picture your success in great detail. Imagine yourself living your dream life. Use your

imagination to create a clear picture of your goals, making them feel real and possible.

7. Make a Plan: Create a clear, actionable plan to reach your goals. Break your big goals into smaller tasks. Set timelines, prioritize what needs to be done, and track your progress regularly.

8. Decide Quickly: Make decisions quickly and with confidence. Avoid being indecisive and procrastinating, as these can stop you from succeeding. Trust your instincts and commit fully to your choices.

9. Keep Going: Don't give up when you face obstacles or failures. See setbacks as chances to learn and grow. Stay

dedicated to your goals, no matter what challenges come your way.

10. Build a Supportive Network: Surround yourself with people who support and inspire you. Create a network of friends, mentors, and collaborators who share your vision and values. Use the collective wisdom and resources of your group to help you succeed.

EXPLORING THE POWER OF POSITIVE THINKING AND MINDSET MASTERY FOR SUCCESS

Positive thinking and having the right mindset are powerful tools for achieving success in all areas of life. They help people build their dreams, overcome challenges, and reach their highest potential.

Positive thinking means looking at the bright side of things. It's about keeping a hopeful attitude and believing in possibilities. Instead of focusing on problems or setbacks, positive thinkers see these as chances to grow and learn. This shift in mindset helps them handle challenges with resilience and determination, leading to more success.

Having the right mindset, or mindset mastery, is closely linked to positive thinking. It means believing strongly in yourself and your abilities, and adopting habits that support personal and professional growth. By mastering their mindset, people can use the power of their thoughts to achieve the results they want.

One of the main benefits of positive thinking and mindset mastery is that they boost motivation and drive. When people have a positive outlook and believe they can succeed, they are more likely to stay motivated and keep going, even when things get tough. This determination helps them overcome obstacles and reach their goals.

Positive thinking and mindset mastery also improve mental and emotional well-being. By focusing on positive aspects of life, people can reduce stress, anxiety, and negativity. This leads to better relationships, health, and overall happiness.

In the workplace, positive thinking and mindset mastery are very important. People who have a positive attitude and a growth mindset are more creative, adaptable, and resilient. They can handle challenges better, take advantage of opportunities, and succeed in today's fast-changing world.

To develop positive thinking and master their mindset, people can practice gratitude, visualization, affirmations, and mindfulness daily. By doing these activities regularly, they can train their brains to focus on the positive, build resilience, and unlock their full potential.

CHAPTER THREE
THE ART OF PERSISTENCE

To get rich by 30, you need more than luck or talent. It takes persistence and a clear plan. It's not about quick money or following trends blindly. Here's how you can do it:

1. Set Clear Goals: Decide what "rich" means to you. Is it having a certain amount of money, financial freedom, or a specific lifestyle? Be clear and realistic.

2. Create a Plan: Break your goals into smaller, manageable steps. Think about what might go wrong and how to handle it. Your plan should be flexible but focused, able to change with circumstances while staying on track.

3.   Take Consistent Action: Wealth doesn't come overnight. It's the result of daily habits and efforts. Stick to your plan, even when progress is slow or you face setbacks. Keep moving forward, one step at a time.

4.   Learn from Failure: Every setback is a chance to learn and grow. Figure out what went wrong, adjust your approach, and keep going. Failure isn't final unless you give up.

5.   Manage Your Finances: Budgeting, saving, and investing are key to building wealth. Spend less than you earn, save money regularly, and invest wisely for the future. Delay some pleasures now for bigger rewards later.

6. Surround Yourself with Supportive People: Find mentors, advisors, and friends who support your goals. Learn from their experiences, ask for advice, and use their knowledge and connections.

7. Stay Focused but Open to Opportunities: Keep your eyes on your goals but be open to new opportunities. Look for new ventures and partnerships. Be curious, adaptable, and willing to step out of your comfort zone. The path to riches is rarely straight, but persistence helps you find new ways to succeed.

8. Believe in Abundance: Trust in your ability to create wealth. Replace negative thoughts with positive ones.

Visualize your success, affirm your goals daily, and stay positive, even when facing challenges.

LEARNING TO PERSEVERE THROUGH CHALLENGES AND SETBACKS ON THE PATH TO SUCCESS

On the journey to success, challenges and setbacks are not just small problems; they are important steps that help shape our character and determination. Learning to keep going through these tough times is essential, often more important than natural talent or intelligence. It's about having grit and resilience to continue when everything seems difficult.

First, it's important to understand that setbacks are normal. They are part of the process, not mistakes. Knowing this can help you see setbacks as chances to grow, not as impossible problems. Instead of feeling discouraged, think of them as lessons to learn from and steps toward your goal.

Second, keeping a positive mindset is crucial. It's easy to feel negative when facing challenges, but staying positive can be powerful. Believe in your ability to overcome problems and face them with a problem-solving attitude. This change in thinking can make a big difference, turning setbacks into temporary roadblocks instead of dead ends.

Perseverance also requires patience. Success rarely happens quickly; it comes from consistent effort over time. Stay committed to your goals, even when progress seems slow. Remember, every step forward, no matter how small, is still progress. Celebrate these small victories to stay motivated.

Additionally, seek support from others. Surround yourself with people who encourage and support you. They can offer good advice, new perspectives, and sometimes just a shoulder to lean on when things get tough. Don't be afraid to ask for help when you need it; it's a sign of strength, not weakness.

Being adaptable is also important. The path to success is often not straight but full of twists and turns. Be ready to change your approach when needed, and see change as a chance to grow. Flexibility helps you handle obstacles better and find new ways to reach your goals.

Lastly, always remember your why. What motivates you to pursue success? Whether it's a passion, a dream, or a sense of purpose, hold onto that motivation during tough times. Let it fuel your determination and remind you why the struggle is worth it in the end.

CHAPTER FOUR

BUILDING STRONG RELATIONSHIPS

1. Honest Communication: Always be honest and open when talking to friends, family, and coworkers. Share your true thoughts, feelings, and dreams to build trust and understanding.

2. Active Listening: Listen carefully to others without interrupting or judging. Pay attention to their words, body language, and emotions. Show that you care about their experiences and views.

3. Empathy and Kindness: Try to understand how others feel by imagining yourself in their situation. Be kind and offer support when they need it.

4. Respect and Appreciation: Show respect by valuing others' strengths and contributions. Appreciate their uniqueness and let them know how important they are to you.

5. Boundaries and Self-Care: Set healthy limits to protect your well-being and respect others' boundaries too. Take care of yourself to stay emotionally balanced and respect others' need for space and independence.

6. Shared Experiences: Spend time together doing activities you both enjoy. Create happy memories through meaningful conversations, fun adventures, and shared hobbies.

7. Conflict Resolution: Disagreements happen in all relationships. Handle conflicts with patience and a desire to understand and compromise. Look for solutions that maintain respect and harmony.

8. Supportive Networks: Surround yourself with supportive friends, mentors, and peers. Rely on them in tough times and celebrate good times together. Keep these relationships strong through regular contact and appreciation.

9. Continual Growth: Always aim to grow and learn from your experiences. Encourage others to pursue their goals and self-improvement too.

10. Gratitude and Celebration: Show thanks to those who make your life better. Celebrate milestones and special moments together. Appreciate the positive role they play in your life.

NURTURING PERSONAL AND PROFESSIONAL RELATIONSHIPS TO SUPPORT YOUR JOURNEY

Building strong connections with family and friends is essential for emotional well-being. Spending quality time with loved ones helps strengthen bonds that provide support during both good times and bad. Sharing your dreams, fears, and achievements with trusted friends and family makes you feel connected and resilient when facing challenges.

Investing in romantic relationships with care and dedication can also bring great happiness and support. Good communication, respect, and understanding with your partner create a strong partnership based on shared goals. Through empathy and compassion, both partners can encourage and motivate each other in personal and professional pursuits.

Fostering professional relationships is key to career growth and new opportunities. Networking with colleagues, mentors, and industry peers allows you to exchange knowledge, insights, and resources. Building a reputation for reliability, integrity, and expertise earns trust and opens doors to new ventures and collaborations.

Seeking mentorship from experienced professionals provides valuable guidance and wisdom. Mentors offer advice, perspective, and encouragement tailored to your goals. A strong mentor-mentee relationship requires active listening, humility, and a willingness to learn and grow from feedback.

Participating in professional communities and associations connects you with like-minded individuals. Engaging in industry events, workshops, and conferences offers opportunities for learning, collaboration, and career advancement. Contributing to these communities through sharing knowledge, mentoring, and supporting others further strengthens relationships and fosters a sense of belonging and camaraderie.

FINANCIAL INTELLIGENCE

1. Budgeting: Make a budget. Keep track of how much money you make and spend. Set aside money for essentials, savings, investments, and fun spending. A budget helps you see where your money goes and makes it easier to make smart money choices.

2. Investing: Start investing as soon as you can. Use the power of compound interest by putting money in stocks, bonds, mutual funds, or real estate. Spread your investments out to lower risk. Learn about different ways to

invest and their potential returns. Keep educating yourself about investment strategies and market trends.

3. Emergency Fund: Save money for unexpected expenses, like medical bills or losing your job. Aim to save at least six months' worth of living expenses in an easy-to-access account. An emergency fund gives you financial security and peace of mind during tough times.

4. Debt Management: Reduce and manage your debt. Pay off high-interest debts, like credit cards, first. If needed, consolidate debts to lower interest payments. Avoid getting into unnecessary debt and try to live within your means.

5. Career Development: Invest in your career. Learn new skills, get advanced education or certifications, and look for chances to move up or get better-paying jobs. Increase your earning potential over time through continuous learning and professional growth.

6. Retirement Planning: Start planning for retirement early. Contribute to retirement accounts like 401(k), IRA, or pension plans. Take advantage of employer matching contributions if available. Consider talking to a financial advisor to create a retirement plan that fits your goals and comfort with risk.

7. Insurance: Protect your money and future earnings with insurance. Get health insurance for medical expenses,

disability insurance to replace income if you can't work due to injury or illness, and life insurance to support your dependents if you die. Review and update your insurance regularly to make sure you have enough coverage.

8. Financial Education: Keep learning about personal finance and investing. Read books, attend seminars, and use online resources to improve your financial knowledge. Stay informed about economic trends and changes that may affect your finances.

CHAPTER FIVE
HEALTH IS WEALTH

At 30, men face a crucial point where their health choices can greatly affect their future. The body might start showing signs of aging, so it needs more care and attention. Focusing on health now is not just about avoiding sickness; it's about building a strong foundation for a happy and active life ahead.

Physical health is key for achieving success and wealth. Regular exercise, whether at the gym, outdoors, or through sports, improves physical fitness, sharpens the mind, and boosts confidence. Eating a balanced and nutritious diet gives the body the energy needed to take on challenges and seize opportunities.

Mental and emotional health is just as important. Work and personal life pressures can cause stress and anxiety if not managed well. Practices like mindfulness meditation, journaling, or getting professional counseling can help handle life's complexities with a clear and resilient mind.

In the quest for success, it's easy to overlook rest and relaxation. However, getting enough sleep and taking time to relax are vital for recharging the body and mind, increasing productivity, and sparking creativity. Balancing work and leisure helps maintain long-term performance and prevents burnout.

Additionally, building meaningful connections and nurturing relationships with family, friends, and mentors makes life richer and provides support during tough times. Being around positive influences and learning from those with similar experiences can speed up personal growth and development.

PRIORITIZING PHYSICAL AND MENTAL WELL-BEING FOR SUSTAINED SUCCESS

Taking care of our physical and mental health is key to long-term success. Success often comes from hard work, but we can't keep performing well if we don't stay healthy.

First, regular exercise is very important. Working out keeps us fit, gives us more energy, and makes us feel happier. Simple activities like walking, running, or stretching can reduce stress and anxiety. Eating a balanced diet is just as crucial. Nutritious food gives us the energy we need to handle our daily tasks better. Getting enough sleep is also important. Good sleep helps our bodies recover and makes our minds sharp, so we can focus and make good decisions.

Mental health is just as important as physical health. Practicing mindfulness and stress management, like meditation or deep breathing, can improve our mental state a lot. Taking breaks during the day to relax can stop us from burning out. It's important to recognize and deal with stress or anxiety instead of ignoring them. Talking to friends, family, or a professional can offer support and new viewpoints.

Balancing work and personal life is also essential. Setting boundaries between work and home helps prevent burnout and ensures we have time to relax and enjoy hobbies. Doing things we enjoy, like reading, playing sports, or spending time with loved ones, makes life more satisfying.

Staying socially connected is very important too. Building and maintaining relationships with friends and family gives us emotional support and a sense of belonging. Joining community activities or groups with similar interests can also boost our social well-being.

LEADERSHIP AND INFLUENCE

At 30, men often reach an important point in their personal and work lives. Being a good leader and having the ability to influence others are key to achieving success and happiness. Good leadership and the power to influence can greatly affect career growth, personal relationships, and overall satisfaction in life.

To lead well at 30, men need a clear vision and a strong sense of purpose. This means setting big but achievable goals and planning how to reach them. At this age, it's important to build self-confidence and improve decision-making skills. Confidence comes from knowing yourself, recognizing your strengths and weaknesses. Decision-making gets better with experience and by being willing to take smart risks.

Influence is about connecting with others on a personal level. Building real relationships is essential. This means listening actively, showing empathy, and communicating effectively. When people feel understood and valued, they are more likely to be positively influenced. Influence is about inspiring and motivating others to achieve shared goals, not about manipulation.

It's crucial to develop a leadership style that is genuine and adaptable. Authentic leaders stay true to their values and principles, gaining trust and respect from others. Being adaptable helps leaders handle different situations and challenges well. At 30, men should aim to be flexible and open to new ideas while staying true to their core beliefs.

Networking is also important for leadership and influence. Building a strong professional network can lead to new opportunities and provide support and guidance. Men should find mentors and role models for advice and learning from their experiences. Being part of a supportive community can enhance one's ability to lead and influence effectively.

Continuous learning and self-improvement are essential. Keeping up with industry trends, learning new skills, and seeking feedback can help men at 30 stay relevant and competitive. Personal growth not only improves leadership abilities but also contributes to overall well-being.

CHAPTER SIX

TURNING ADVERSITY INTO ADVANTAGE

Life is full of challenges and setbacks that can feel overwhelming and disheartening. However, tough times can also help us grow and succeed if we have the right mindset. The key is to see difficult experiences as chances to learn and improve.

One of the most important steps in turning tough times into advantages is to stay positive. It's normal to feel down when things go wrong, but keeping a hopeful attitude can help us cope and succeed. By seeing challenges as temporary and fixable, we can focus on solving problems instead of feeling stuck.

Another important aspect is resilience. Being resilient means having the mental and emotional strength to bounce back from setbacks. We can build resilience by setting realistic goals, having a support network of friends and family, and taking care of ourselves. Resilience helps us stay strong and motivated, even when things don't go as planned.

Learning from tough times is also essential. Each setback teaches us valuable lessons that can help us improve and avoid similar problems in the future. Reflecting on what went wrong and finding areas for growth can turn a negative experience into a stepping stone for success. This requires honesty and a willingness to accept responsibility, but it leads to greater self-awareness and personal growth.

Adaptability is another key factor. Being able to change our strategies and approaches when things change is vital for overcoming challenges. This might involve learning new skills, seeking advice from others, or being open to new ways of thinking. Flexibility helps us navigate through difficulties effectively and come out stronger.

Lastly, perseverance is essential. Persistence in tough times can make the difference between giving up and achieving success. By staying committed to our goals and continuing to push forward, we can overcome obstacles and reach our desired outcomes.

GOAL SETTING AND ACTION PLANNING

Goal setting and action planning are important skills for personal and professional growth. They help you create a clear path to reach your goals and keep you focused and motivated. Here's a simple guide to understanding and using these strategies effectively.

Goal Setting

1. Define Clear Goals: Start by clearly defining what you want to achieve. Make sure your goals are specific, measurable, achievable, relevant, and time-bound (SMART). For example, instead of

saying "get fit," say "run 5 kilometers in under 30 minutes within three months."

2. Break Down Goals: Big goals can feel overwhelming. Break them into smaller, manageable tasks. For example, if your goal is to write a book, aim to finish one chapter each month.

3. Set Priorities: Not all goals are equally important. Decide which goals are the most important and focus on those first. This way, you put your energy and resources into what matters most.

4. Write Down Your Goals: Writing your goals down makes them real and keeps them in front of you as a

reminder. This can help you stay committed.

Action Planning

1. Identify Necessary Actions: Once you have your goals, list all the actions needed to achieve them. Include every step, even the small ones, that will help you reach your goal.

2. Create a Timeline: Set deadlines for each action. This helps you keep moving forward and ensures steady progress. For instance, if you need to complete a project in six months, set deadlines for each task monthly or weekly.

3. Allocate Resources: Figure out what resources you need, such as time, money, or help from others. Properly

allocating resources is essential for your plan to succeed.

4. Monitor Progress: Regularly check your progress to stay on track. You can do this with weekly check-ins or monthly reviews, depending on how complex your goal is. Adjust your plan as needed to overcome any challenges.

5. Stay Flexible: Be ready to adapt your plan if things change. Flexibility helps you deal with unexpected obstacles without losing sight of your goals.

CRAFTING A MEANINGFUL LEGACY THAT TRANSCENDS FINANCIAL SUCCESS

1. Share What Matters to You: Tell people about your beliefs and values. Write letters, make videos, or keep a journal explaining what you believe in and why. Share stories from your life that show these values in action.

2. Build Strong Relationships: Spend time with family, friends, and colleagues. Show them love, respect, and kindness. Be there for them, offer support, and stay involved in their lives. These strong connections will help spread your influence.

3. Mentor Others: Teach and guide others, especially younger people. Share

your knowledge and experiences. Offer advice, encouragement, and support. Your guidance can help shape their futures and continue your impact.

4. Help Your Community: Get involved in your local community. Volunteer, support local projects, or start your own initiatives to address local needs. Your efforts can improve the lives of others and build a lasting sense of community.

5. Support Education: Help educational efforts by donating, providing scholarships, or volunteering your time. Education empowers people and communities, and your support can create opportunities for future generations.

6. Stand Up for Important Issues: Advocate for causes that matter to you, like protecting the environment, social justice, or healthcare. Use your voice and resources to drive change and raise awareness. Your advocacy can inspire others and lead to lasting improvements in society.

7. Be Generous: Give not just money, but also your time, skills, and attention. Acts of kindness and generosity can spread goodwill and inspire others to do the same.

8. Create Something Lasting: Make something that reflects your passions, like art, writing, music, or a business. Your creations can inspire, educate, and

bring joy to others even after you're gone.

THE END

www.ingramcontent.com/pod-product-compliance
Lightning Source LLC
Chambersburg PA
CBHW050023230526
45470CB00003B/1106